Relationship Keeper Series©

KEEP STRONG TOGETHER
Relationship Quotes for Adult Coloring & Couples' Workbook

Dr. Patt Pickett, LMFT, MEd, PhD
Wisdom of *The Marriage Whisperer*®

Outside-the-Box Books
St. Louis

Keep Strong Together: Relationship Quotes for Adult Coloring & Couples' Workbook
Imprint of The Relationship Keeper Series©

Other imprint products include expert self-help books, full-size workbooks, and coloring books. All books are supported further by resource card decks, classes/online Date Night WebClasses. Individual/Couple/Group online video sessions by appointment.

Original Quotes created by Dr. Patt Pickett, PhD
Written and created by Dr. Patt Pickett PhD
Worksheets created by Dr. Patt Pickett PhD
Edited by Mary Horner
Interior Art created using Fiver.com
Interior Layout by Brad Cook
Cover Design by Brad Cook

www.PattPickett.com

ISBN: 978-1-7365312-0-4
Adult Coloring | Inspirations-Quotes |Expert Relationship Tips | Self-Help | Marriage Workbook

Outside-the-Box-Books

Outside-the-Box Books is dedicated to providing high quality and professionally developed self-help resources for ALL individuals, marriages, relationships, committed unions, and families. We realize that we cannot be perfectly correct for everyone. Nevertheless, we value sensitivity, respect, inclusion and work to avoid gender bias and references as best we understand.

    • For qualified wholesale purchases & fulfillment: www.IngramSpark.com.

    • Available for retail purchase at gift shops, bookstores, and at IndieBound.org (for the locations of independent bookstores in your area) along with Amazon, Barnes & Noble, and other online sources.

    • For discounts on quantity retail purchases (book clubs, schools, hospitals, treatment centers, art therapy groups, licensed therapists, meditation groups, and more), contact the publisher directly to discuss.

Outside-the-Box Books
10820 Sunset Office Drive, Suite 204
St. Louis, MO 63127
877-447-3262
DrPatt@PattPickett.com

Praise for Keep Strong Together

"Dr. Patt Pickett's book, "Keep Strong Together" delivers insightful relationship quotes embedded in a clever design for adult coloring. The workbook is great for starting couple's conversations".

Eva Harster, MBA, President and Certified Virtual Expert, More Time to Profit, LLC

"I was totally impressed with the professional combination of unique quotes and application of the "how to" apply to my own relationships. I'm always on the lookout for expert resources that are simple and practical. The coloring book adds fun to learning the tips and tools."

Gina Baldwin, M.S., CCC-SLP, Speech Language Pathologist

Help & Contact Information

The author, Patt Pickett, PhD is a licensed mental health provider. Her professional experience and training provide the background for the relationship quotes and homework in this coloring book. However, Dr. Patt is not YOUR counselor. Reading and acting on the information in her books and products does not constitute a counselor/client relationship.

Ideas, Q&A, homework, quotes, and all information contained here are presented for the purposes of independent self-help, fun, enrichment, and education.

This book is NOT a substitute for counseling, coaching, consulting, or any professional contact including spiritual, legal, criminal justice services, or the medical advice of physicians. Readers should regularly consult a physician in matters relating to their health and particularly with respect to any symptoms that may require diagnosis or medical attention.

If you are
- being verbally or emotionally abused
- in danger of physical harm from yourself or others
- in emotional distress
- being assaulted
- having any other emergency

Please contact professional services, dial 911 (or your local emergency #), OR go immediately to the nearest hospital emergency room. Ask for help....YOU deserve it!

Free Emergency Help Lines
(Published as of May 2021)

National Suicide Prevention Lifeline 1-800-273-8253
National Alliance on Mental Illness-NAMI (Weekdays during business hours) 1-800-273-8255
National Help Hotline (24/7-365 days/year) 1-800-662-4351

Non-Emergency Mental Health Resources
A few sources to locate a Mental Health provider in your area:

- Go to TherapistLocator.net
- Contact your state local division of professional registration
- Ask a trusted relative or friend for a referral
- Consult your primary care provider (PCP).

How Did This Coloring Book Come Alive?

As I made this coloring book, I recovered a fond childhood memory I want to share. At 12, my highly prized possessions were a 64-count, flip-top box of Crayola Crayons, a huge collection of colored pencils, and a box of pastels which I saved and have shown to my baffled grandkids. (Why would Gramma save — THIS?) In my defense, I don't have any of the Crayola Crayons first produced in 1903 in an 8-count box selling for 5 cents. I am headed for... but not even close to — 100 years old yet. To continue my story, as a kid, I always tried being sneaky to cleverly hide those coveted tools of my art. I was determined to keep all six of my siblings, one was older and five younger, from "borrowing" some. I seldom succeeded.

Thirty years ago, I bought a tin of Crayola Collector's Colors, Limited Edition for $5 on sale. According to the information included on the tin (which is still unopened), in 1958, the company had introduced what was then its largest box. It had a count of 64 and a built-in sharpener ... just like the one I loved!

This copyrighted 1991 tin contained a box of 8 colors — maize, raw umber, blue gray, lemon yellow, green blue, orange yellow, orange red, and violet blue — which were retired from the classic color assortment and inducted into the Crayola Hall of Fame in 1990. Those colors were replaced in the 64-count box, also in the tin, eight bright new colors — dandelion, wild strawberry, vivid tangerine, fuchsia, teal blue, royal purple, jungle green, and cerulean.

By now you know ... I have always loved art and coloring — the calm, the joy, the creativity. And for the past 34 years as a licensed therapist, I have followed my passion for helping people reach their happy and best relationships and marriages. With this coloring book, I have combined my passions.

Invitation to Share Your Calm, Joy, & Creativity
on the Coloring Page with Your Favorite Quote

Hello, Everyone,

There are endless possibilities to creative coloring. Whether you are an experienced colorist or newbie, your work is unique regardless of the process. The style, order, colors, strokes, and more represent YOU. We'd love for you to share with us the coloring page that you completed which is on your favorite slice of relationship wisdom. Tell us why that quote is the most meaningful to you. (Narrative is preferred but optional.)

1.   Once a month or as determined by the volume of responses, we will select from all pages received. As a thank you to our valued customers, discount coupon codes toward one of our products or services will be e-mailed to each creator-author of the pages that we select from those received. (Discount codes will expire, are not transferrable, may only be used once, and have no cash value.)

2.   By sending us your favorite to share, you understand and agree that your coloring page and narrative become the property of Dr. Patt Pickett with all rights including commercial attached. Any response may be selected and used for commercial purposes by Dr. Patt Pickett without further permission or any compensation or recognition to the sender/creator-author. However, you will be notified if possible if your page/narrative is selected for use. PLEASE NOTE: We reserve the right to edit your narrative for clarity and acceptability.

3.   If the sender is NOT also the creator-author, they must include with the material a specific release signed by the creator-author granting release of all rights to Dr. Patt Pickett, as explained in #2 above.

4.   All submissions shared must include your name and can only be selected/accepted when sent via a valid e-mail address to **DrPatt@PattPickett.com**. By submitting via e-mail, you consent for that address to be added to our e-mailing list for information, updates, Dr. Patt's newsletter, and product/service availability. We will not sell/give away your information.

5.   Discount coupon code offers will expire without further notice. However, submissions will continue to be accepted when received and used as determined appropriate. For updated information, updates, and questions regarding the invitation to share contact **DrPatt@PattPickett.com**

I personally thank you very much for your purchase. Please spread the good word.

Warmly.
Dr. Patt

Please use the open pages for your own quotes, doodles, and notes.

Name: :Name

&

WILL
KEEP STRONG
TOGETHER

SWEAT The small STUFF Before it BUILDS a bonfire.

A SILVER anniversary TOGETHER is not a MERIT BADGE for health OR HAPPINESS.

SHARING GROWTH WITH YOUR PARTNER GROWS YOUR RELATIONSHIP.

DO NOT SETTLE FOR A LIFE TOGETHER BY DEFAULT. SET GOALS.

Relationships CREATE one COUPLE Of two PEOPLE.

Uniqueness DOES NOT create conflict. . Stubbornness & lack of COMMUNICATION DO.

BE AN ATTENTIVE LISTENER. YOU WILL LEARN SOMETHING.

Ask clarifying questions. Do not assume you have it right.

SEE THE DIFFERENCE BETWEEN INFLUENCE & CONTROL. LET YOUR PARTNER'S FEELINGS & OPINIONS MATTER.

PLAY TOGETHER to STAY TOGETHER.

LOVING SHRINKS WHEN YOUR LIFE IS REMOTELY CONTROLLED.

If you want
to
grow older
together,
don't
let things
grow old.

We have not communicated until what I meant--- is what YOU understood.

It is the second person to speak who starts the argument.

Change
is not a
four-letter
word.
S-A-M-E
is.

PASSION MISAPPLIED IS CONTROL.

RELATIONSHIPS ARE A 60/60 PROPOSITION. DO YOUR 60%

We all have the same 24/7. What we do with our time becomes our priority.

LIFE IS TOO LONG
TO BE MISERABLE
& TOO SHORT
TO WASTE.

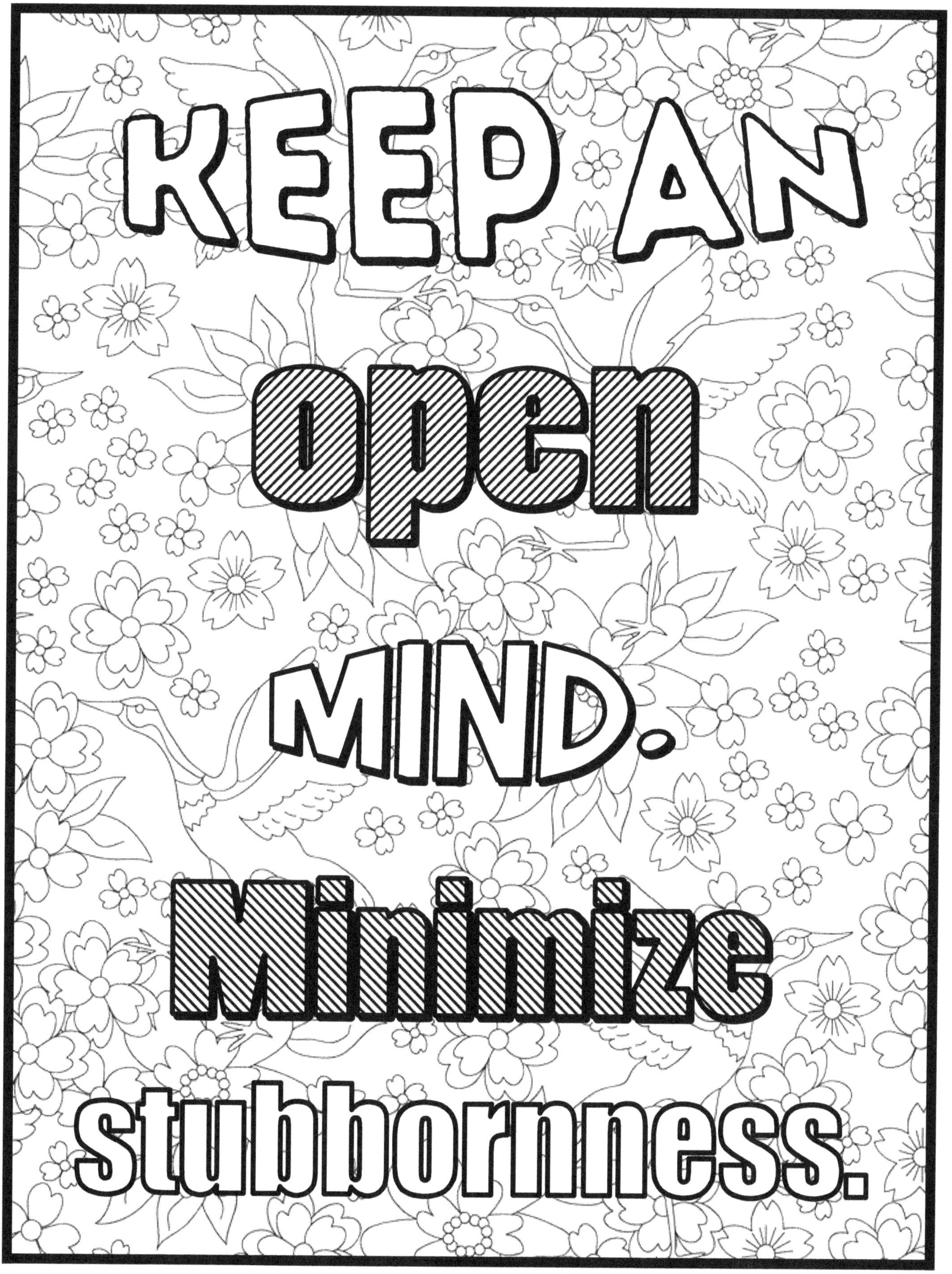
KEEP AN
open
MIND.
Minimize
stubbornness.

Relationship Keeper Series©
Keep Strong Together

Mini-Workbook

Copy 1 of 2 for _____

The Relationship Keeper Series©
Keep Strong Together

WORKBOOK*

Name_____

Date_____

Name_____

Date_____

Do your homework & keep strong together. Ask your partner to share in coloring the pages and/or complete the mini-workbook page independently. Invite them to join in relationship conversations with you.

There are four types of homework for you to complete:

- ♥ *Slices of Relationship Wisdom Check List*
- ♥ *Marriage and Relationship Inventory*
- ♥ *Quizzes for Starting Relationship Conversations*
- ♥ *Action Plan to Keep Strong Together*

When you are coloring/sharing the coloring, relax but also be mindful of the wisdom soaking in through your senses. Read the quotes aloud. Spell as you color each word to become mindful and hear what you are learning. Your thinking, visual, and tactile senses engage with each color choice and stroke.

If you pass on coloring, appreciate your partner's creativity and hobby. Comment on what you like and accept the other's invitation to join in conversation. (And if you were not invited, think about why not and consider a self-invitation.)

Heads Up: These suggestions for how to do the homework are guides to get you started. Use the homework as tools and uniquely adapt them to YOUR special relationship. The goal is not to put triangles into rectangles. Find the relationship place you both accept as best for you individually and as a couple together.

For more help and information on relationships, check out all The Relationship Keeper Series© products especially the Keep Strong Together, 7 Habits of Great Couples, expanded workbook, resources, Date Night Web Class and visit www.PattPickett.com for additional products and services.

The Relationship Keeper Series©
Slices of Wisdom

CHECK LIST for HABITS to keep strong together. *First, each partner should read all tips independently.*

Compare/contrast answers with each other. Discuss every tip with open minds & create understanding. Explore how/if each fits in your life together.

Check as many reactions as you have. Add totals for each column.	LIKE IT	BELIEVE IT	DOUBT IT	DOING IT	UNSURE /OTHER
1. Keep strong together.					
2. Sweat the small stuff… before it builds a bonfire.					
3. A silver anniversary together is not a merit badge for health or happiness.					
4. Sharing growth with your partner grows your relationship.					
5. Do not settle for a life together by default. Set goals.					
6. Relationships create one couple of two people.					
7. Uniqueness does not create conflict. Stubbornness & lack of communication do.					
8. Be an attentive listener. You will learn something.					
9. Ask clarifying questions. Do not assume you have it right.					
10. See the difference between influence & control. Let your partner's feelings & opinions matter.					
11. Play together to stay together.					
12. Loving shrinks when your life is remotely controlled.					
13. If you want to grow older together, don't let things grow old.					
14. We have not communicated until what I meant--- is what you understood.					
15. It is the second person to speak who starts the argument.					
16. Change is not a four-letter word. S-A-M-E is.					
17. Passion misapplied is control.					
18. Relationships are a 60/60 proposition. Do your 60%.					
19. We all have the same 24/7. What we do with our time becomes our priority.					
20. Life is too long to be miserable & too short to waste.					
21. Keep an open mind. Minimize stubbornness.					
TOTALS					

The Relationship Keeper Series©
INVENTORY

Marriage and Relationship

CIRCLE how strongly you agree or disagree with these statements.

A. *Overall, I feel our marriage/relationship is strong.*
1. STRONGLY AGREE 2. AGREE 3. UNSURE 4. DISAGREE 5. STRONGLY DISAGREE

B. *We handle our conflicts and disagreements without excessive anger or any disrespect.*
1. STRONGLY AGREE 2. AGREE 3. UNSURE 4. DISAGREE 5. STRONGLY DISAGREE

C. *We set goals for our life together.*
1. STRONGLY AGREE 2. AGREE 3. UNSURE 4. DISAGREE 5. STRONGLY DISAGREE

D. *We play together often enough.*
1. STRONGLY AGREE 2. AGREE 3. UNSURE 4. DISAGREE 5. STRONGLY DISAGRE

E. *Neither of us spends too much leisure time with phone/video chats, social media, online gaming, TV/streaming series, sports watching, or similar technology habits.*
1. STRONGLY AGREE 2. AGREE 3. UNSURE 4. DISAGREE 5. STRONGLY DISAGREE

F. *Overall, I feel we do a fairly equal share of couple/family work & other responsibilities.*
1. STRONGLY AGREE 2. AGREE 3. UNSURE 4. DISAGREE 5. STRONGLY DISAGREE

G. *I feel the love I need from my partner.*
1. STRONGLY AGREE 2. AGREE 3. UNSURE 4. DISAGREE 5. STRONGLY DISAGREE

H. *My partner feels the love they need from me.*
1. STRONGLY AGREE 2. AGREE 3. UNSURE 4. DISAGREE 5. STRONGLY DISAGREE

TOTALS: _____ STRONGLY AGREE _____ AGREE _____ UNSURE ____ DISAGREE _____ STRONGLY DISAGREE

- ✓ Count the total # of each response. If you have more than 2 "UNSURES"...why?
- ✓ Compare and contrast answers with your partner.
- ✓ Explore any pattern of answers.
- ✓ Identify strengths and weaknesses. Plan actions to use strengths and reduce weaknesses.
- ✓ Address any surprise answers from your partner. Disappointments?
- ✓ Are you unable to complete a discussion together about this inventory and/or the rest of the homework? If so, seriously think about seeking professional relationship/marriage counseling or coaching services to gain communication skills to talk about your relationship openly, honestly, and productively. Your relationship will gain strength and closeness----with even a little effort. Consider the possibility.

The Relationship Keeper Series©
QUIZZES

Start Your Relationship Conversations

Study each of the 21 tips. Keep in mind your initial reactions you marked on the check list. Complete your answers separately from your partner. Plan together a scheduled time to start and finish a relationship conversation around each one of the quizzes.

Here are 4 suggestions for scheduling your talks:

1. 1 tip/day for 3 weeks.
2. 3 tips/day for 1 week
3. 7 tips/weekend for 3 consecutive weeks
4. 1 three+ hour time slot (SOON) to discuss all 21 tips (not recommended)
5. You be creative with what works best for you both.

Obvious recommendations… or maybe NOT

Keep an open mind and maintain respect during your conversations. Create a relatively balanced give-and-take of talking/listening. This will be difficult for some couples. Work at it. Have fun. Accept surprises and disappointments. Know it is common that, as individuals, you two may have different experiences of how pleasant or helpful each of the discussions are.

Consider committing to a "time-out/time-in" agreement for if this happens. The person who calls the "time-out" is responsible (right then) for setting up a specific and agreeable "time-back-in" with their partner. The partner accepting the "time-out" from the other then stays "chill" until the designated "time-back-in". Remember, this can only be a successful tool when both partners honor their commitments. Accepting an unwanted "time-out" may never happen again if the "time-outer" does not come through with the "time-back-in" as promised.

Write any pre-conversation agreements you may find helpful or necessary:

_____

_____

_____

_____

The Relationship Keeper Series©

1.Keep Happiness Together.

What first popped into your mind when you read this?

_____

_____

How and why does this apply or not apply to your relationship?

_____

_____

_____

Will you and your partner agree on this? _____

NOTES_____

2. Sweat the small stuff… before it builds a bonfire.

What first popped into your mind when you read this?

_____

_____

How and why does this apply or not apply to your relationship?

_____

_____

Will you and your partner agree on this? _____

NOTES_____

3. A silver anniversary together is not a merit badge for health or happiness.

What first popped into your mind when you read this?

_____

_____

_____

How and why does this apply or not apply to your relationship?

_____

_____

Will you and your partner agree on this? _____

NOTES_____

4. Sharing growth with your partner grows your relationship.

What first popped into your mind when you read this?

_____

_____

How and why does this apply or not apply to your relationship?

_____

_____

Will you and your partner agree on this? _____

NOTES_____

5. Do not settle for a life together by default. Set goals.

What first popped into your mind when you read this?

_____

_____

How and why does this apply (or not) to your relationship?

_____

_____

Will you and your partner agree on this? _____

NOTES_____

6. Relationships create one couple of two people.

What first popped into your mind when you read this?

_____

_____

How and why does this apply or not apply to your relationship?

_____

_____

Will you and your partner agree on this? _____

NOTES_____

The Relationship Keeper Series©

7. Uniqueness does not create conflict.
Stubbornness & lack of communication do.

What first popped into your mind when you read this?

_____

_____

How and why does this apply or not apply to your relationship?

_____

_____

Will you and your partner agree on this? _____

NOTES_____

8. Be an attentive listener. You will learn something.

What first popped into your mind when you read this?

_____

_____

How and why does this apply or not apply to your relationship?

_____

_____

Will you and your partner agree on this? _____

NOTES_____

The Relationship Keeper Series©

9. Ask clarifying questions. Do not assume you have it right.

What first popped into your mind when you read this?

_____

_____

How and why does this apply or not apply to your relationship?

_____

_____

_____

Will you and your partner agree on this? _____

NOTES_____

10. See the difference between influence & control.
Let your partner's feelings & opinions matter.

What first popped into your mind when you read this?

_____

_____

How and why does this apply or not apply to your relationship?

_____

_____

Will you and your partner agree on this? _____

NOTES_____

The Relationship Keeper Series©

11. Play together to stay together.

What first popped into your mind when you read this?

_____

_____

How and why does this apply or not apply to your relationship?

_____

_____

_____

Will you and your partner agree on this? _____

NOTES_____

12. Loving shrinks when your life is remotely controlled.

What first popped into your mind when you read this?

_____

_____

How and why does this apply or not apply to your relationship?

_____

_____

Will you and your partner agree on this? _____

NOTES_____

The Relationship Keeper Series©

13. If you want to grow older together, don't let things grow old.

What first popped into your mind when you read this?

_____

_____

How and why does this apply or not apply to your relationship?

_____

_____

Will you and your partner agree on this? _____

NOTES_____

14. We have not communicated until what I meant--- is what you understood.

What first popped into your mind when you read this?

_____

_____

How and why does this apply or not apply to your relationship?

_____

_____

Will you and your partner agree on this? _____

NOTES_____

15. It is the second person to speak who starts the argument.

What first popped into your mind when you read this?

_____

_____

How and why does this apply or not apply to your relationship?

_____

_____

Will you and your partner agree on this? _____

NOTES_____

16. Change is not a four-letter word. S-A-M-E is.

What first popped into your mind when you read this?

_____

_____

How and why does this apply or not apply to your relationship?

_____

_____

Will you and your partner agree on this? _____

NOTES _____

The Relationship Keeper Series©

17. Passion misapplied is control.

What first popped into your mind when you read this?

_____

_____

How and why does this apply or not apply to your relationship?

_____

_____

Will you and your partner agree on this? _____

NOTES_____

18. Relationships are a 60/60 proposition. Do your 60%.

What first popped into your mind when you read this?

_____

_____

How and why does this apply or not apply to your relationship?

_____

_____

_____

Will you and your partner agree on this? _____

NOTES_____

The Relationship Keeper Series©

19. We all have the same 24/7. What we do with our time becomes our priority.

What first popped into your mind when you read this?

_____

_____

How and why does this apply or not apply to your relationship?

_____

_____

Will you and your partner agree on this? _____

NOTES _____

20. Life is too long to be miserable & too short to waste.

What first popped into your mind when you read this?

_____

_____

How and why does this apply or not apply to your relationship?

_____

_____

Will you and your partner agree on this? _____

NOTES _____

The Relationship Keeper Series©

21. Keep an open mind. Minimize stubbornness.

What first popped into your mind when you read this?

_____

_____

How and why does this apply or not apply to your relationship?

_____

_____

Will you and your partner agree on this? _____

NOTES _____

SUMMARY NOTES

What are your relationship goals and what changes do you need to make to get there?

_____
_____
_____
_____
_____
_____
_____
_____
_____
_____
_____
_____
_____
_____
_____
_____

MORE SUMMARY NOTES

The Relationship Keeper Series©

ACTION PLAN to KEEP STRONG TOGETHER

Recipe for Success: *Be clear. Be simple. Be strong. Be consistent.*

Name _____   Name _____

To Do Date(s)	Intent and goal of Change	Describe Details of Actions and Communications	Initials	Long Term or Done Date

Relationship Keeper Series©
Keep Strong Together

Mini-Workbook

Copy 2 of 2 for _____

The Relationship Keeper Series©
Keep Strong Together

WORKBOOK*

Name_____

Date_____

Name_____

Date_____

Do your homework & keep strong together. Ask your partner to share in coloring the pages and/or complete the mini-workbook page independently. Invite them to join in relationship conversations with you.

There are four types of homework for you to complete:

- ♥ *Slices of Relationship Wisdom Check List*
- ♥ *Marriage and Relationship Inventory*
- ♥ *Quizzes for Starting Relationship Conversations*
- ♥ *Action Plan to Keep Strong Together*

When you are coloring/sharing the coloring, relax but also be mindful of the wisdom soaking in through your senses. Read the quotes aloud. Spell as you color each word to become mindful and hear what you are learning. Your thinking, visual, and tactile senses engage with each color choice and stroke.

If you pass on coloring, appreciate your partner's creativity and hobby. Comment on what you like and accept the other's invitation to join in conversation. (And if you were not invited, think about why not and consider a self-invitation.)

Heads Up: These suggestions for how to do the homework are guides to get you started. Use the homework as tools and uniquely adapt them to YOUR special relationship. The goal is not to put triangles into rectangles. Find the relationship place you both accept as best for you individually and as a couple together.

For more help and information on relationships, check out all The Relationship Keeper Series© products especially the Keep Strong Together, 7 Habits of Great Couples, expanded workbook, resources, Date Night Web Class and visit www.PattPickett.com for additional products and services.

The Relationship Keeper Series©
Slices of Wisdom

CHECK LIST for HABITS to keep strong together. *First, each partner should read all tips independently.*

Compare/contrast answers with each other. Discuss every tip with open minds & create understanding. Explore how/if each fits in your life together.

Check as many reactions as you have. Add totals for each column.	LIKE IT	BELIEVE IT	DOUBT IT	DOING IT	UNSURE /OTHER
1. Keep strong together.					
2. Sweat the small stuff… before it builds a bonfire.					
3. A silver anniversary together is not a merit badge for health or happiness.					
4. Sharing growth with your partner grows your relationship.					
5. Do not settle for a life together by default. Set goals.					
6. Relationships create one couple of two people.					
7. Uniqueness does not create conflict. Stubbornness & lack of communication do.					
8. Be an attentive listener. You will learn something.					
9. Ask clarifying questions. Do not assume you have it right.					
10. See the difference between influence & control. Let your partner's feelings & opinions matter.					
11. Play together to stay together.					
12. Loving shrinks when your life is remotely controlled.					
13. If you want to grow older together, don't let things grow old.					
14. We have not communicated until what I meant--- is what you understood.					
15. It is the second person to speak who starts the argument.					
16. Change is not a four-letter word. S-A-M-E is.					
17. Passion misapplied is control.					
18. Relationships are a 60/60 proposition. Do your 60%.					
19. We all have the same 24/7. What we do with our time becomes our priority.					
20. Life is too long to be miserable & too short to waste.					
21. Keep an open mind. Minimize stubbornness.					
TOTALS					

The Relationship Keeper Series©
INVENTORY

Marriage and Relationship

CIRCLE how strongly you agree or disagree with these statements.

A. Overall, I feel our marriage/relationship is strong.
1. STRONGLY AGREE 2. AGREE 3. UNSURE 4. DISAGREE 5. STRONGLY DISAGREE

B. We handle our conflicts and disagreements without excessive anger or any disrespect.
1. STRONGLY AGREE 2. AGREE 3. UNSURE 4. DISAGREE 5. STRONGLY DISAGREE

C. We set goals for our life together.
1. STRONGLY AGREE 2. AGREE 3. UNSURE 4. DISAGREE 5. STRONGLY DISAGREE

D. We play together often enough.
1. STRONGLY AGREE 2. AGREE 3. UNSURE 4. DISAGREE 5. STRONGLY DISAGRE

E. Neither of us spends too much leisure time with phone/video chats, social media, online gaming, TV/streaming series, sports watching, or similar technology habits.
1. STRONGLY AGREE 2. AGREE 3. UNSURE 4. DISAGREE 5. STRONGLY DISAGREE

F. Overall, I feel we do a fairly equal share of couple/family work & other responsibilities.
1. STRONGLY AGREE 2. AGREE 3. UNSURE 4. DISAGREE 5. STRONGLY DISAGREE

G. I feel the love I need from my partner.
1. STRONGLY AGREE 2. AGREE 3. UNSURE 4. DISAGREE 5. STRONGLY DISAGREE

H. My partner feels the love they need from me.
1. STRONGLY AGREE 2. AGREE 3. UNSURE 4. DISAGREE 5. STRONGLY DISAGREE

TOTALS: _____ STRONGLY AGREE _____ AGREE _____ UNSURE _____ DISAGREE _____ STRONGLY DISAGREE

- ✓ Count the total # of each response. If you have more than 2 "UNSURES"...why?
- ✓ Compare and contrast answers with your partner.
- ✓ Explore any pattern of answers.
- ✓ Identify strengths and weaknesses. Plan actions to use strengths and reduce weaknesses.
- ✓ Address any surprise answers from your partner. Disappointments?
- ✓ Are you unable to complete a discussion together about this inventory and/or the rest of the homework? If so, seriously think about seeking professional relationship/marriage counseling or coaching services to gain communication skills to talk about your relationship openly, honestly, and productively. Your relationship will gain strength and closeness----with even a little effort. Consider the possibility.

The Relationship Keeper Series©
QUIZZES

Start Your Relationship Conversations

Study each of the 21 tips. Keep in mind your initial reactions you marked on the check list. Complete your answers separately from your partner. Plan together a scheduled time to start and finish a relationship conversation around each one of the quizzes.

Here are 4 suggestions for scheduling your talks:

1. 1 tip/day for 3 weeks.
2. 3 tips/day for 1 week
3. 7 tips/weekend for 3 consecutive weeks
4. 1 three+ hour time slot (SOON) to discuss all 21 tips (not recommended)
5. You be creative with what works best for you both.

Obvious recommendations... or maybe NOT

Keep an open mind and maintain respect during your conversations. Create a relatively balanced give-and-take of talking/listening. This will be difficult for some couples. Work at it. Have fun. Accept surprises and disappointments. Know it is common that, as individuals, you two may have different experiences of how pleasant or helpful each of the discussions are.

Consider committing to a "time-out/time-in" agreement for if this happens. The person who calls the "time-out" is responsible (right then) for setting up a specific and agreeable "time-back-in" with their partner. The partner accepting the "time-out" from the other then stays "chill" until the designated "time-back-in". Remember, this can only be a successful tool when both partners honor their commitments. Accepting an unwanted "time-out" may never happen again if the "time-outer" does not come through with the "time-back-in" as promised.

Write any pre-conversation agreements you may find helpful or necessary:

_____

_____

_____

_____

The Relationship Keeper Series©

1.Keep Happiness Together.

What first popped into your mind when you read this?

_____

_____

How and why does this apply or not apply to your relationship?

_____

_____

_____

Will you and your partner agree on this? _____

NOTES_____

2. Sweat the small stuff... before it builds a bonfire.

What first popped into your mind when you read this?

_____

_____

How and why does this apply or not apply to your relationship?

_____

_____

Will you and your partner agree on this? _____

NOTES_____

The Relationship Keeper Series©

3. A silver anniversary together is not a merit badge for health or happiness.

What first popped into your mind when you read this?

_____

_____

_____

How and why does this apply or not apply to your relationship?

_____

_____

Will you and your partner agree on this? _____

NOTES_____

4. Sharing growth with your partner grows your relationship.

What first popped into your mind when you read this?

_____

_____

How and why does this apply or not apply to your relationship?

_____

_____

Will you and your partner agree on this? _____

NOTES_____

The Relationship Keeper Series©

5. Do not settle for a life together by default. Set goals.

What first popped into your mind when you read this?

_____

_____

How and why does this apply (or not) to your relationship?

_____

_____

Will you and your partner agree on this? _____

NOTES_____

6. Relationships create one couple of two people.

What first popped into your mind when you read this?

_____

_____

How and why does this apply or not apply to your relationship?

_____

_____

Will you and your partner agree on this? _____

NOTES_____

The Relationship Keeper Series©

7. Uniqueness does not create conflict.
Stubbornness & lack of communication do.

What first popped into your mind when you read this?

_____

_____

How and why does this apply or not apply to your relationship?

_____

_____

Will you and your partner agree on this? _____

NOTES_____

8. Be an attentive listener. You will learn something.

What first popped into your mind when you read this?

_____

_____

How and why does this apply or not apply to your relationship?

_____

_____

Will you and your partner agree on this? _____

NOTES_____

The Relationship Keeper Series©

9. Ask clarifying questions. Do not assume you have it right.

What first popped into your mind when you read this?

_____

_____

How and why does this apply or not apply to your relationship?

_____

_____

_____

Will you and your partner agree on this? _____

NOTES_____

10. See the difference between influence & control.
Let your partner's feelings & opinions matter.

What first popped into your mind when you read this?

_____

_____

How and why does this apply or not apply to your relationship?

_____

_____

Will you and your partner agree on this? _____

NOTES_____

The Relationship Keeper Series©

11. Play together to stay together.

What first popped into your mind when you read this?

_____

_____

How and why does this apply or not apply to your relationship?

_____

_____

_____

Will you and your partner agree on this? _____

NOTES_____

12. Loving shrinks when your life is remotely controlled.

What first popped into your mind when you read this?

_____

_____

How and why does this apply or not apply to your relationship?

_____

_____

Will you and your partner agree on this? _____

NOTES_____

The Relationship Keeper Series©

13. If you want to grow older together, don't let things grow old.

What first popped into your mind when you read this?

_____

_____

How and why does this apply or not apply to your relationship?

_____

_____

Will you and your partner agree on this? _____

NOTES_____

14. We have not communicated until what I meant--- is what you understood.

What first popped into your mind when you read this?

_____

_____

How and why does this apply or not apply to your relationship?

_____

_____

Will you and your partner agree on this? _____

NOTES_____

15. It is the second person to speak who starts the argument.

What first popped into your mind when you read this?

_____

_____

How and why does this apply or not apply to your relationship?

_____

_____

Will you and your partner agree on this? _____

NOTES_____

16. Change is not a four-letter word. S-A-M-E is.

What first popped into your mind when you read this?

_____

_____

How and why does this apply or not apply to your relationship?

_____

_____

Will you and your partner agree on this? _____

NOTES _____

The Relationship Keeper Series©

17. Passion misapplied is control.

What first popped into your mind when you read this?

_____

_____

How and why does this apply or not apply to your relationship?

_____

_____

Will you and your partner agree on this? _____

NOTES_____

18. Relationships are a 60/60 proposition. Do your 60%.

What first popped into your mind when you read this?

_____

_____

How and why does this apply or not apply to your relationship?

_____

_____

_____

Will you and your partner agree on this? _____

NOTES_____

The Relationship Keeper Series©

19. We all have the same 24/7. What we do with our time becomes our priority.

What first popped into your mind when you read this?

_____

_____

How and why does this apply or not apply to your relationship?

_____

_____

Will you and your partner agree on this? _____

NOTES _____

20. Life is too long to be miserable & too short to waste.

What first popped into your mind when you read this?

_____

_____

How and why does this apply or not apply to your relationship?

_____

_____

Will you and your partner agree on this? _____

NOTES _____

The Relationship Keeper Series©

21. Keep an open mind. Minimize stubbornness.

What first popped into your mind when you read this?

_____

_____

How and why does this apply or not apply to your relationship?

_____

_____

Will you and your partner agree on this? _____

NOTES _____

SUMMARY NOTES

What are your relationship goals and what changes do you need to make to get there?

_____
_____
_____
_____
_____
_____
_____
_____
_____
_____
_____
_____
_____
_____
_____
_____

MORE SUMMARY NOTES

ACTION PLAN to KEEP STRONG TOGETHER

Recipe for Success: *Be clear. Be simple. Be strong. Be consistent.*

Name _____ Name _____

To Do Date(s)	Intent and goal of Change	Describe Details of Actions and Communications	Initials	Long Term or Done Date

Copyright 2021 Patt Pickett, PhD   All Rights Reserved www.PattPickett.com

Message from the Author

Hello, Colorists and Readers.

Thank you for purchasing my coloring book with a workbook. This is a new project for me, and I would love to get your feedback for the future mini-workbook I have planned. Please drop me an e-mail directly OR post a review on your favorite site, and let me know where to find it. If you are a coloring fan, spread the word to the other hobbyists you know.

When you sign-up for my mailing list, I will send you a Relationship Keeper Series © Packet with the list of tips for how to be "Married for a Lifetime" and the "Top 10 Reasons You Know You are Not Wrecking Your Marriage". You can also visit my Facebook Live broadcasts on WiseAce360, and hear me discuss those relationship tips and more.

My Best Regards,
Dr. Patt

DrPatt@PattPickett.com

About the Author

During well over 10,000 hours throughout her 30+ years of professional experience, the author, Dr. Patt Pickett, SEICC, LMFT, MEd, PhD, also known as The Marriage Whisperer®, has worked in her mental wellness practice specializing in marriage, relationships, family, communication, and emotional intelligence.

Dr. Patt is state licensed as marriage and family therapist providing services in coaching |consulting | and counseling | to couples| families | and individuals. She is also state certified as a teacher and presents workshops and webinars. Prior to becoming a counselor, Dr. Patt served in the government as a probation and parole officer for 13 years. * Considering her experience, people frequently comment, "Bet you have seen and heard it all!" Her humble reply is, "Nope, only lots of it."

Dr. Patt is well-known for her 'outside-the-box thinking'. When she encourages her clients and others "to consider the possibility …", they frequently respond, "I never thought about it that way before". She has earned a solid reputation for infusing her practical, non-judgmental approaches with warm guidance, directness, and energy --- often with respectful snark and humor.

As co-owner of St. Louis Emotional Intelligence (EQ) Center, she offers two thoroughly research-based online assessments. Dr. Patt is a Social and Emotional Certified Coach (SEICC) through the Institute for Social and Emotional Intelligence (ISEI). The EQ assessment she offers was developed by the ISEI, takes about 20 minutes, and includes downloadable results and a self-help guide for improvement. Dr. Patt completed in-person, Level 2 Training in Gottman Method Couples' Therapy (32 hours). She offers an online assessment for a couples' check-up created by Drs. John and Julie Gottman. The Gottman Relationship Check-up automatically scores a relationship's strengths and challenges and provides specific recommendations for intervention. More information about both online assessments can be found at www.PattPickett.com .

The author is an accomplished writer. Her work includes published and well-received/ award-winning self-help relationship books, #1 International Bestseller, popular newspaper/ magazine articles, and advice columns. She creates personal/relationship development resources including card decks and podcasts/videos. Her media achievements include expert guest appearances on local TV/radio.

Dr. Patt was raised by her parents as second of seven children. Her mom was a homemaker who took care of the kids and caught the dust before it landed. Her dad worked hard outside their home to provide the basics. Today, she and her husband have five children and nine grandkids. Together, they enjoy regular couple time, family, and activities --- board/card games, golf, gardening, travel, and home entertaining, and her solo hobby time is artwork, sewing, and gourmet cooking. She is known to quip, "I never met a French fry I did not like."

Among many life challenges she has personally faced, Dr. Patt won against workplace sex discrimination*, beaten cancer, and renewed her life drive and passions after traumatic loss of right eye vision.

Dr. Patt continues to spread her message of optimism and encouragement to all who listen that life change, relationship growth/improvement, and happiness are possible for those who are motivated and do the work.

Publisher

Outside-the-Box Books is an indie publisher focused on self-reflection, understanding, and positive change. Our coloring books for adults are filled with life and relationship quotes written by an expert, Dr. Patt Pickett. As a bonus for couples, our "quotes" coloring books include a mini-workbook (in duplicate) loaded with self-help, stress relief, relaxation, mindfulness/ meditation, irony, and humor.

Our mission is presenting simple tips and tools for practical personal and relationship development provided by a mental wellness professional. Coloring books are part of the Relationship Keeper Series (RKS), which includes, a companion to this coloring book, *Keep Strong Together: 7 Habits of Great Couples*, a short and easy self-help book. RKS also offers workbooks, card decks, and plans many more products and services to come.

Outside-the-Box Books is grateful and delighted for the chance to offer you exciting wellness resources to enjoy while learning.

Contact Us

Stay updated and connected with what we are up to next by visiting our website and join our email list at www.PattPickett.com .

* Details of Dr. Patt's story of sex discrimination and harassment as a probation and parole officer with the US Courts are in her personal narrative and poem, "Why Can't I?", which appear in the anthology, *"Living My tRuth – Personal Reflections on the Impact of the RBG Legacy"*, A Compilation by Cathy L. Davis (June 2021), available in e-book and paperback.

Relationship Keeper Series© products include:

Adult Coloring Books

Wellness Resource Card Decks

Expert Self-Help Books

Series Workbooks

Date Night WebClasses

Sold Separately

PattPickett.com

Relationship Keep Series©

Keep Strong Together

7 Habits of Great Couples

Discover all the Relationship Keeper Series resources including the companion coloring book Keep Strong Together: Relationship Quotes for Adult Coloring & Couples' Workbook

Enter the zone to earn your
7 LOVE BADGES

What are "love badges"?
They are awards for progress in growing stronger in your marriage or relationship. By completing the fun and simple experiences with your partner, you will ---

- Increase your closeness.
- Forget about being "right". Focus on influence.
- Find 17 ideas to set relationship goals.
- Understand your partner's "love tells".
- Discover 5 anti-stress ideas.
- Root out "unfairness" as a relationship "weed".

ISBN: 978-1-7365312-1-1
Marriage | Expert Relationship Tips | Inspirations-Quotes
Isolation | Self-Help | Crisis Stress Tips

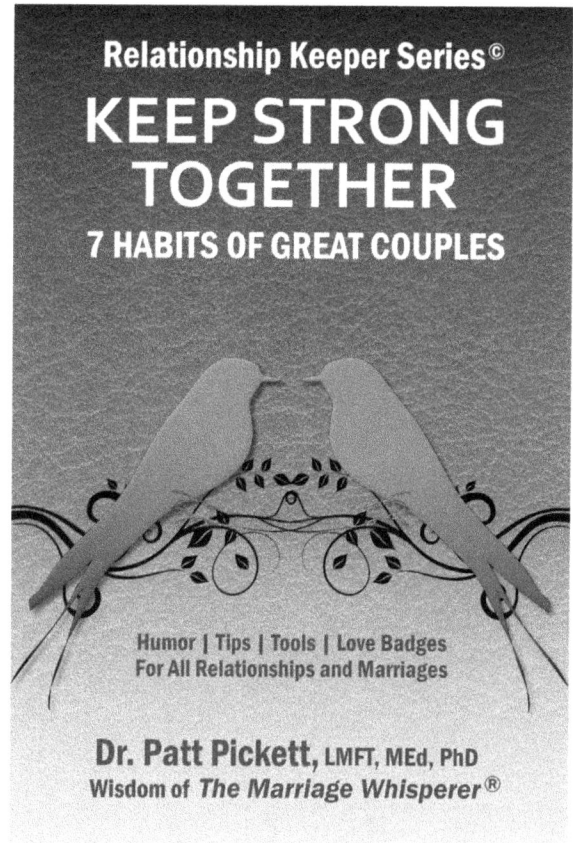

Relationship Keeper Series©
KEEP STRONG TOGETHER
7 HABITS OF GREAT COUPLES

Humor | Tips | Tools | Love Badges
For All Relationships and Marriages

Dr. Patt Pickett, LMFT, MEd, PhD
Wisdom of *The Marriage Whisperer*®